REFLECTIONS

Of

CHRISTMAS

Edited by Fiona Stevenson

ISBN 978-1-4717-5770-9

These stories were written by the Stevenson's,

William, Kerry and Fiona.

We hope that you will enjoy them.

But more than that –

We pray that you too will sing the angel's song,

"Glory to God in the Highest.."

because

"God so loved the world, that He gave His only begotten Son, that whosoever believeth in Him should not perish, but have everlasting life."

God bless you.

As,

at this time,

we celebrate the birth of the Saviour,

the Lord Jesus Christ,

we pray that your hearts will be warmed

by His grace, His humility,

the gift of His wonderful love.

May you carry into, and through, the coming year the assurance of His loving presence, His guiding hand, and His abiding glory.

CONTENTS

Short, short stories, these were all written as entries for a Writing Challenge. One or two of the events are biographically based, but none of the characters represent any living person. We all enjoyed writing them and pray that you will enjoy as much reading them, sharing with us memories of yesteryears but most of all, the true magic that is expressed in the love of God for each one of us.

CHRISTMAS IS COMING

FDS

"Christmas is a-coming, the geese are getting fat; won't you please drop a penny in the old man's hat?"

It was springtime, with its warm, gusty winds and influenza. With the washing safely pegged and blowing on the line, I found the strength to pull a few weeds and rake a patch of leaves. Underneath the wild strawberries clustered dark leaves round bright berries. Without a voice to speak – my throat was jammed with splintered wood – I stroked a congratulation to the Painted Ladies who at last had discovered their beauty to the world around. I looked with longing at the loveliness about me, the tasks that needed to be done, but my small reserve of strength was gone. I wobbled back indoors.

It is time to post the greeting cards to precious people overseas. The cards, the lists, are pushed aside. I cannot concentrate. Leaning back, I close my eyes, watching faces drift back more than fifty years to the first

Christmas of really celebrating the birth of the Saviour, of knowing who this Baby was, why He was born. A Christmas that had little to do with geese getting fat, or with pennies dropped in an old man's hat...

The church went carolling on Christmas Eve. It was before the dark days of litigation and expensive insurance claims. On this, and several subsequent years, we hired a flatbed two-ton truck, loaded a pedal-pump organ and thirty or forty stacking chairs. The bodies occupying them would hold them in place. We took carol books and music and loads of fun and laughter. Our organist doubled as a teacher at a Mission Station out of town. She had a Master's Degree in Theology. To us she was Anna who played the 'pianna' and the young people adored her and teased her.

The pastor phoned the hospitals and aged care homes arranging times for us to visit and sing. We had to leave the truck and organ. Anna led the singing, using her music book as a baton.

We sang up the hills and through the twisting streets of the suburbs, stopping at the homes of friends. Last of all, we drove along the main street of the town where revellers were gathered on the warm hotel verandas. Usually this was where we met our most vigorous response. Requests were shouted, sung with cardboard throats and great gusto, the crowd joining in. Pastor Dan preached an impromptu gospel of the great Good News from the tailboard of the truck.

It was close to midnight before we wandered home, still singing snatches of the carols, chuckling about incidents of the evening. Then, because this was our tradition, it was time to decorate the house and dress the Christmas tree. There were always many hands to hang the tinsel and 'snow' the Christmas tree with cotton wool, to place the presents underneath. We drank a sea of coffee and ate a hill of snacks before our pillows claimed us for an hour or two of sleep.

Christmas day. The faithful came to sing the songs of triumph, to adore the name of Jesus, to salute the happy morn. We shared the gladness of the men of old who beheld the shining star. And we sang the words of Scripture: '... unto us a Child is born, unto us a Son is given ...' while we broke bread at the foot of the tree that became a cross. We bowed the knee to the Lamb of God and sang with the herald angels, ‘All glory to the new-born King!’

At home again we cut the Christmas cake and sang, ‘Happy birthday, Jesus’ while we opened the gifts from under the tree. Laughter and paper littered the room. Other gifts and other loves took temporary precedence.

Another meal was served. We ate the turkey and the trimmings, the custard and the pud. We took our tea and coffee to easy chairs and somnolence while the children admired and tried their new toys or read their new books. The radio played a selection of Christmas music. The Spirit stirred among the words of the carols, turning our thoughts to the feast of bread and wine, the greatest Gift of all, the Babe lying in a manger, the Son given that we might have life – abundant life.

For God so loved the world,

that He gave His only begotten Son,

that whosoever believeth in Him should not perish,

but have eternal life.

For God sent not His Son into the world to condemn the world;

but that the world through Him might be saved.

He that believeth on Him is not condemned:

but he that believeth not is condemned already

because he hath not believed in the name of the only begotten Son of God.

Gospel of John 3:16 KJV

THE WONDER OF IT ALL

WS

"Gabriel, I want you to go to earth again. This time I want you to visit a virgin in Nazareth and tell her that I have chosen her to bear my son."

"I am aware of your promises to Israel, your elect," said Gabriel, "but I don't understand why all this is necessary."

"You don't need to know. My secrets keep the enemy guessing as well. Satan can only act after the events, which gives us the upper hand."

Gabriel winged his way down to earth, to the village of Nazareth, to the home of the young maiden, Mary. He thought, 'Mary is of the family line of David to whom the Messiah is promised, while King Herod is a political ring-in. Good choice, God, but this Joseph is only a carpenter. True, he too is of David's line. I guess God knows what He is doing.'

Arriving in Mary's presence, Gabriel startled her with his greeting, "Hail! You are highly favoured among women!"

Mary showed her fear at this sudden intrusion into her daily affairs, and wondered what kind of greeting this was.

"Don't be afraid, Mary. God has chosen you to bring his son into this world – you will become pregnant and the Messiah will be born."

"How can this be? I have not been with a man."

"No, no. The Holy Spirit of God will overshadow you and implant his seed in you. That is why your child will be the son of God. You must have heard that your cousin, Elizabeth, who has been barren all her life, is now pregnant and is in her sixth month. I must go now."

Excitedly, Mary hurried to Joseph's house. "Joseph, I have been visited by an angel, and I am pregnant!"

"Mary, Mary, don't be foolish! You can't be pregnant – we have not been together yet!"

"No, Joseph, this is different: God is giving me this child."

"Mary, go back home and say nothing to anyone else. I'll sort the matter out favourably."

After Mary left, Joseph pondered, 'Mary is a good girl, however she became pregnant. She needs me to protect her from scandal. I cannot marry her, so I'll give her a bill of divorcement privately. Only the Elders will know.'

That night Joseph tossed and turned in his bed, his concern for Mary was great. In a dream an angel visited him, "Joseph, you must not hesitate to take Mary for your wife. The child she has conceived is really from God."

Joseph woke and realising his dream was from God determined to marry Mary. He advised her, "Go and visit your cousin Elizabeth. Be out of town for a while."

On her arrival, Elizabeth greeted her, "It is really a privilege for me to be visited by the mother of the Messiah. I know, because as soon as I heard your voice, my baby jumped for joy in my womb." Mary stayed with Elizabeth until it was time for John to be born.

Returning to Nazareth Mary heard that the Roman governor had decreed that every resident of Israel must go to the city of their family line to register. Both Mary and Joseph, being descendants of David, would have to register in Bethlehem when the time came.

As is the way with women, Mary's child grew in her womb and would be due just about the time they needed to travel and register. Although concerned, they travelled to Bethlehem.

Bethlehem was crowded. The inns were full and Joseph and Mary were forced to sleep in a cave set aside for the animals. Mary's baby was born there, and she wrapped him in loose cloths and laid him in the manger.

"Gabriel, take some angels with you, it's time to announce the birth of my son."

Once again Gabriel sped to earth, to Bethlehem. He was not alone this time. He spotted some shepherds on the hills near the city and decided to tell them.

Those shepherds were astounded to be visited by angels. Over the last four hundred years no one had heard from heaven, they seemed to be brass. Gabriel told the shepherds the good news and the other angels sang in praise to

God, “Glory to God, and on earth peace to those who will receive His good will.”

The shepherds rushed into the city and found the good news to be true. They went from house to house telling all who would listen.

X x X x X

Behold, a virgin shall conceive,

and bear a son,

and they shall call his name

IMMANUEL.

Isaiah 7:14 KJV

CHRISTMAS CARD REMINDER

FDS

"Oh, look, darling, here's one from Auntie Joan."

I took the card she put into my hand, wondering idly who Auntie Joan was. It was a pretty card with three tall candles on the front. I placed it with the other cards on the table beside the bed.

"I'm thirsty."

She brought a glass of water.

"Thank you, nurse." As I raised the glass to my mouth a thought occurred to me. "This water has been boiled, hasn't it, nurse?"

She replied in a muffled voice, "Yes, Mrs. O. I made sure it was boiled this morning. It is quite safe."

I relaxed and drank. Cholera is a terrible disease. So ravaging.

I watched her stand Auntie Joan's card among the small forest of paper. She was an attractive girl, very kind, very attentive. She must be a 'special' – she seemed to be always near. Hospitals had changed, too. I was very tired, but not so tired that I couldn't appreciate the quiet luxury of this private room, the soft furnishings and filmy curtains. I closed my eyes and let the pillows hold me, felt the gentle tapered fingers soothe the hair at my temples. "Sleep a little, Gram, I'll take you for a walk when it gets cooler."

I strode through the long, open ward, crowded and jumbled with dark-skinned patients. The outbreak had been severe, the mission hospital not equipped for the numbers or the severity of the epidemic. There was little rest for the staff. The doctors were hollow-eyed with exhaustion. The school was closed. The teachers came in as nurse-aids. Joan was the tall one, dark haired, dark eyed, always laughing. It almost seemed she loved the children back to life. She met each challenge with a smile, no task demeaned her. I alone shared her tears. We prayed together, digging through the Psalms for comfort, seeking guidance from the words of Jesus. We saluted each morning with Paul's greeting, "Grace be with you."

Joan, fellow-soldier, faithful friend.

At last, the worst was over. Patients left on their feet, not via the morgue. We straightened up and thought about normality. Someone looked at the calendar. "Would you look at that! Only a week left to Christmas!"

One of the teachers went to town and came back with a bulging postbag. "Come along, everyone, Christmas cards galore!"

We pinned the cards around the walls to decorate the hospital, singing carols while we worked. We found a small tree for the dining room, tied bandage bows, 'snowed' it with cotton wool. In place of lights we used cotton buds dipped in Mercurochrome, Gentian violet and acriflavine.

I woke, holding fast the precious memory. Pushing myself up on the pillows, I reached for Joan's card. Three precious Lights – Father, Son and Holy Ghost. I opened it and read, "Dear Fellow-soldier, I have been thinking of our cholera-Christmas so many years ago, and wondering how many more years we will have to celebrate the Saviour's birth before He comes again. Just so you know it is really me thinking of you – Grace be with you. Joan."

As I replaced her card among the others, granddaughter Sheryl came through the door. Reaching for her hands I smiled at her. "Sheryl, precious girl, I have been forgetting so much lately. So before I forget again, I want to thank you very much for your love and care, and to wish you a very happy Christmas. And may His grace and peace be always with you."

CHRISTMAS IN RHODESIA

WS

"Listen, folks, this year Christmas falls at the weekend, giving us at least four days free from our workplaces to celebrate the birth of Jesus Christ. How about a church family camp?"

The 'amen's' echoed all around the congregation, from young and old. Theirs was a Pentecostal congregation who understood that 'amen' meant 'so let it be,' and so it would be.

The plans began. "For Christmas day we will have a braai. After all, we won't have a white Christmas no matter who tries to dream one up."

The pastor was a well-built Irishman who had come to Rhodesia as a missionary. His congregation was made up of people from all over the world. Many of the members had experienced the Welsh revival, the rest were local converts. This lively congregation was like a great big family because they had left their homelands to come to Rhodesia.

After the service you could hear Iris calling, "Over by here, ladies, we need to plan the Christmas baking for our camp. It won't be Christmas without the fare."

So the ladies gathered while the men chatted over cups of tea and scones.

"I can make Christmas cake enough for all," that was little Patty from Liverpool. "My Mum always made enough to feed the five thousand and I've got her recipes."

"We won't have that many!" Iris responded.

"I just love making tarts. Lemon curd and berry both go well at Christmas. I think I'll need help if we are going to have everyone come." Agnes was an Afrikaner.

"I'll tell you what. Let's get together on Thursday nights between now and the camp to report on how things are going. We've got two months."

"Won't that be difficult for you, Anna?" Anna was a missionary from the Old Umtali Mission at Penhalonga and attended the church for her own spiritual growth.

"Sometimes. But I can contact Iris by phone. Two months is not very long. I'll make shortbread from a real Scots recipe."

With such enthusiasm and willingness the baking would soon be under control.

The elders and deacons met that same night to plan the logistics and details of the camp.

"Let's make the Christmas eve fellowship a time of 'Carols around the camp-fire' with more than one song leader so that no one tires." Young Billy was a youth leader in the making, and the young ones loved singing.

"Sure. But Idris should train a choir to do some specials for us." Howard interjected.

Idris, Iris' husband, was from Wales and always prepared the congregation for carol singing at Christmas. His favourite stories were, "Did you know that Jonah was a Welshman? To be sure, for Welshmen sing - and pray – in Wales (whales)." And, "Did you know that Yul Brynner was jealous of Moses? Because he had Aaron (hair on)." Everyone loved Idris.

"On Christmas day we should start the day with prayer and praise before breakfast for about half an hour," the pastor suggested.

"Yes, and after breakfast we can have a time of testimonies of what God has done for us over the year – with tea and cookies!"

"You young ones are always thinking of your stomachs! Testimonies first. Tea and cakes later."

"What about the main Christmas message?"

"I think we should invite Jason Mataringa to address us."

Jason was the local African minister. He had once been the church cleaner. His enthusiastic witness to both black and white visitors to the church had led the congregation to send him to Bible College, and now he had a congregation of his own in the local African township.

"Yes, his congregation should be invited to join us. Their singing and harmony always blesses us."

All was agreed, and when Christmas arrived the two congregations joined in the camp, giving due regard to the segregation laws of

Rhodesia. The Christmas beetles sang their shrill carols all day long.

The braai was the men's responsibility; the mutton chops, steaks and sausages were grilled on the barbeque with onions. The African women prepared a 'sadza,' a thick porridge made from maize meal. The ladies made salads, and the Christmas lunch served under the bright branches of the Flamboyant trees with Poinsettia decorations on the trestle tables, was enjoyed by all.

As the two pastors gave thanks for God's bountiful provision, not only of food, but more importantly for the gift of His only true Son, a great weekend of Christian fellowship was enjoyed by all.

We wish you a merry Christmas

and a happy new year.

AMANDA'S CHRISTMAS CARD

LKS

Amanda felt her loneliness as she sat at her dressing table, teasing the brush through her hair on that sunny afternoon. It had been three years since her two "Freddies" had died in that horrible accident.

It was not supposed to have happened. Their newborn baby was barely a month old when Freddy had gone for a walk through the shopping centre, proudly carrying baby Freddy in the crook of his left arm, head resting in his hand, and feet barely reaching the bend of his elbow, snugly wrapped against the weather. That drunk driver had clipped the inside of the roundabout, mounted the sidewalk at the intersection, and run right over them from behind. Amanda shuddered at the shock she felt when she heard of the accident, and tears welled in her eyes as she pictured the conversation at her unit door. It was so unexpected, so ... so horrible! She choked a stifled sob.

Now she sat alone, tearfully toying with the brush in her hands. How she missed Freddy. If only she could hear him say he loved her once more. He was so tender at times she could feel his passion for her in the tone of his voice. Her frame shook as she remembered how she missed him so.

“Oh, Freddy,” she said wistfully, looking at the bedroom ceiling, “if only you could say you love me once more.” Was it never to be?

Rising from the dressing stool she walked from the bedroom, still thinking of Freddy. She remembered how often he studied her fingers. “What’s wrong?” she would ask.

Breaking from his thoughts he answered, “Oh, nothing. Don’t worry about it. Let’s go.” He always mentioned some thing or some place, smiled, and said, “I love you, Beautiful” as he dragged her along to his bidding. She smiled sadly and went to look for post.

It was close to Christmas and she found a card re-routed from her family home. It had come via the dead letter office. Looking at the post date she wondered how it had managed to survive all these years and reach her now. Five long years had passed since it was originally sent.

As Amanda entered the unit she thought she recognised the writing, and her hands began to tremble. Reaching for a butterknife she prised the envelope open and extracted the Christmas card within. As she did so something fell to the floor. She bent and picked up the eternity ring that lay at her feet. Opening the card she read, “My dear Amanda, merry Christmas. I will always love you, forever. Freddy.”

Amanda gasped and began to sob. She clutched the card and ring to her breast as she staggered across the living room. Too emotional to sit, she wandered around the room, crying, laughing, and crying some more. Looking through tear filled eyes at the Christmas scene pictured, she pressed the card to her lips and held it there, and then began to dance.

Finally, exhausted from wildly swinging emotions, she found a needle and thread, and sewed the ring to the card. Sweeping all the other cards from the sideboard into a drawer, she stood Freddy’s card alone as a centrepiece. She would not wear the ring till Christmas day.

When Christmas Day finally arrived Caroline, her closest friend, visited to bring some cheer to Amanda's Christmas. They ate, drank, and chatted a while till Caroline, who could not keep from glancing at the lonely card on the sideboard, went over to it and said, "It's a little sad to see only one card standing here."

A smiling Amanda crossed the room, picked up the card and pulled the ring from it. Sliding the ring onto her finger, she replied, "It's the only one that matters."

Looking at her fingers spread in front of her she said to the room, "Look, Freddy, it fits perfectly, and it really does matter. I will love you always and forever, too. Thank you, darling, for a most perfect Christmas."

She turned and wept into Caroline's shoulder.

• * * * * * *

The WORD became flesh ... Master became servant ... CREATOR became man ... Perfection became sin so that old would be new, death would be life ... slave would be heir ... sorrow would be joy ...

OF CULTURE AND TRADITION

FDS

Two heads were bent close together: an unruly auburn mop and a smooth chocolate swirl. Spread across the table were opened cookery books.

"Look at this – this looks absolutely yummy..."

"Mmm, yes, but this is a sure-fire recipe – never known it to fail..."

"I think we should try something different this year..."

"Yes, okay, but Christmas is supposed to be traditional..."

"Sure, but whose tradition?"

Sister-snatches of conversation, while recipes were picked out, perused, set aside or discarded. It was October, time to bake the Christmas cake, time to plan the Yule tide fare.

"Right, then, we'll use your never fail recipe for the cake – only let's add some nuts. When shall we shop? This afternoon? We'd better make a list."

"No, we'll photocopy the recipe and take it with us."

"Might as well shop for the pudding and the fruit mince as well."

"Yes. Have you got those recipes?"

"Somewhere here."

The chocolate swirl moved around the table, lifting up books, shuffling the recipes around.

"Here's a pudding." She passed the recipe across the table.

The auburn mop shook. "No. You want the one with the grated carrot in the mix. I think the fruit mince is in the same book. It should be an old one, hardcover ..."

The recipes were copied, the shopping was done. During the following week the cakes were baked, the puddings steamed and the fruit mince packed into jars. Steeped in the aroma of the fruit and the ambience of a task complete, the girls leaned back in easy chairs, tired feet resting on the coffee table, sipping steaming cups of lemon tea. After several years of separation the sisters worked together easily, each enjoying the others company.

Setting aside her empty cup and stretching luxuriously the chocolate swirl asked, “When do we ice?”

“Week after next, I think.”

“Which shops stock marzipan?”

The auburn mop straightened in shock.

“Marzipan? Bought marzipan? We don’t buy marzipan.” She took a deep breath and enunciated slowly and clearly, biting off each word. “We – make – almond – icing!”

The chocolate swirl hugged herself and chuckled. “Gotchya, didn’t I? And we make the fudge and the Turkish Delight, and the cookies, and the punch, and, and, and...”

Her sister looked at her with disfavour. “You don’t have to make anything it it’s too much trouble. I will.”

"Ah, come on, sis. Lighten up a bit. We'll make them together and have fun doing it." She leaned over and ruffled her sister's already unruly mop. "You don't get to lick all the bowls clean, greedy thing!"

November drew to a close. The cakes were iced, the candies made. Once more the books were opened, the heads bent over them together.

"How many people?"

"Twelve or fourteen, I think."

"Your table won't seat that many."

"No. We'll get a trestle and some folding chairs."

"What do we serve? Traditional fare?"

"Not altogether. My oven wouldn't cope. We'll do some hot, some cold. That way people have more choices and I don't have to worry about who likes what."

"Brilliant idea. Do you remember the Christmas with Auntie Alice when she decided that we would send the money we usually spent on Christmas food to the orphans in some forgotten corner of the world, and we feasted on sandwiches and cordial?"

"Oh, yes! And the Christmas when Uncle Cecil..."

Busy fingers made lists while the memories ebbed and flowed. Turkey, fish, sliced meats, a leg of pork. Potatoes, pumpkins, parsnips, and a long list of salad stuff. Setting aside the chosen recipes they packed the books back on the shelf, and fastened the lists to the refrigerator door with magnets.

"We'll do the big shop and make the cookies next week, then we'll do the final shop a few days before Christmas. Only three weeks now and it will all be over."

"And we'll be considering new diets for the New Year. Why do we eat so much at Christmas? I am quite sure all this could not have been further from Mary's mind as she rode into Bethlehem. We really do make gods of our bellies, don't we, sis?"

They sang an old song, linking arms in an impromptu pirouette, feet avoiding the furniture, turning and swaying as they danced.

“But we all like figgy pudding,

Oh, we all like figgy pudding,

Yes, we all like figgy pudding,

So bring some out here!”

The chocolate swirl bowed, the auburn mop curtsied, and they quoted in mirthful unison, “And we won’t go until we get some!”

MERRY CHRISTMAS!

LKS

I couldn't think of a single thing to write for the competition I thought of entering.

"It's a dumb topic," I told my son. "Christmas lights! Can't they think of something more meaningful?"

Five minutes later I began telling him this tale.

Merry Christmas.

It was extremely early on Christmas morn ....
I was awakened with a yawn.

I suppose it was the cool breeze blowing through the open window and under the fluttering curtain. I shivered and pulled the cover up, then lay there wandering through my thoughts.

It came to me suddenly: "It's Christmas!"

Wanting to be the first to open presents, I leapt out of bed and rushed to the top of the stairs – and tripped over Ginger, a very lazy, very fat cat.

“Aaargh!”

Thud, thud,

Thud, thud,

Thump, thump,

Thud, thump,

Thud, thud,

Thump!

- It’s a twelve story building, you realise -

Thump, thump,

Thump, thud,

Thud, thump,

Thud, thud,

And thud,

And thump!

Pant, puff, pant, pant!

It's tiring trying to make this up to one hundred and fifty words –

Thud, thud,

Thump,

And thud!

"Uurgh!" I lay at the bottom of the stairwell looking up through glazed eyes and realised I could see the colourful lights of Christmas spinning slowly round my sore head.

And that's the best – or worst – I could come up with!

God bless.

CHRISTMAS REVELRY

WS

It was Christmas eve and the city sidewalks gleamed with brightly coloured lights as the shops enticingly displayed their wares to those passing by. “Come and buy our dainties,” they cried to those looking on. “Something special for your lady-love!” or “Isn’t this just the thing for your beau?” Many items were greatly reduced in price because the hour was getting late. Whatever you desired could be had for a reduced price.

Not all who passed by were shoppers; some were merely curious, some window-shoppers, noting bargains they hoped to snap up in the January sales, and many others were just lost in the revelry with little regard to the reason for the season.

A banner boldly proclaimed: ‘JESUS IS THE REASON FOR THE SEASON’ to all who would read, but many revellers were too far gone to care. Especially Tim, who was weaving a very crooked path along the sidewalk. Tim was an average young man who would celebrate at any excuse. His evening had been spent imbibing alcohol to create in him the spirit of Christmas. If it had not been for the constant emphasis on religion at this time he would not have realised that there was any connection.

On various street corners church groups stood singing Christmas carols, praising their God for the coming of His Son, Jesus Christ, into this world. Tim approached one of these groups and getting close to a pretty young lady, said, “Come on, darling, let you and I go celebrate Christmas together. I’ll give you a real good time. Leave these old fuddy-duddies, you and I can really make things hop.”

Carol drew away, but inwardly she felt sorry for this lost soul. “Not tonight.”

She remembered how a year ago she too had thought that revelling was having a happy Christmas. That was before she found new life in Jesus.

Tim staggered on into the night and Carol thought she may never see him again. She prayed, “Father, if it be possible, let that boy find salvation.”

The group continued carolling and at midnight decided to go home. They would meet again in the morning to celebrate the Saviour’s birth afresh. Carol didn’t have far to go and the streets were still very well lit despite the closing of the shops. She felt perfectly safe covering the short distance to her home alone. There was one short stretch past a park, but she would hasten by and it would be perfectly alright. As she sped up Carol heard a sob in the hedge and saw two feet sticking out.

Should she pause to look? Would she be safe? Would her father be angry? O Lord, what should I do? She stooped to look and there before her eyes was Tim, the young man who had approached the carollers. His head was cut and he needed help.

(Serves him right, you say? He got drunk.)

Carol pulled her mobile phone from her pocket and called her father. “Dad, come quick. I’m by the park and I need help!”

Her father needed no second invitation. He ran from the house covering the one hundred and fifty yards to the park in record time. He was thinking as he ran, "I hope Carol is safe." "If anyone harms my little girl they'll have me to deal with!" "I can't see anyone with her..."

Relieved to see that his daughter was safe he set to helping the young man at her feet. They took Tim to their home and contacted his family after finding his identity and phone number in his wallet.

Tim spent the night with Carol's family and found himself in their church next morning, carolling with those he had mocked the night before. The pastor told the Christmas story of how Jesus had left the ivory palaces of heaven and been born in a stable to fulfil the prophecies. He told of how the angels proclaimed His birth in a manger in Bethlehem as the One born to be Saviour of all who would believe.

It was with great gusto that Tim sang, "Joy to the world, the Lord has come..." His head ached with the hangover, but he was happy with his new found friends, even though he still wasn't sure about all this Jesus stuff.

CHRISTMAS TREES DON'T HAVE BUTTONS

FDS

"Christmas trees don't have buttons, darling." His grandmother laughed at Jamie. The chocolate soldier mutinied, his lower lip jutting forward. He looked very fierce.

"Yes, they does."

He selected a bright green button from a wonderfully coloured fistful of chocolate beans. Mrs. Hazeltine watched in amusement. Would it join its fellows on the tree or become another smudge upon a chubby cheek. The table was cluttered with pans, cookie cutters and biscuit dough. Jamie had charge of the chocolate beans for buttons, the raspberry straps and tiny chocolate chips for the faces of the gingerbread men. He had decorated all the gingerbread men and started on the Christmas trees while his grandmother cut the stars and lambs to decorate the real tree.

"Did my mummy help you with your baking, Granny?" Jamie busied himself with the task of buttoning the Christmas trees. He didn't look up. Mrs. Hazeltine paused briefly, studying the intent face.

"Yes, Jamie," she answered gently. "Your mummy loved to put the faces and the buttons on the gingerbread men. Christmas was her favourite time of year."

"Me too!" Jamie flashed an enchanting smile. "I wish Jesus could be born all over again and I would be a shepherd and bring Him a lamb."

Mrs. Hazeltine laughed. "Your mummy wanted almost the same thing, Jamie, only she wanted to be an angel and sing the best carol."

Jamie fixed a button in the almost centre of each star and gave each lamb a chocolate eye before the trays slid into the oven.

As they tidied the table and washed the cutters Mrs. Hazeltine remembered the night, now two years ago, when Jamie came to live with her. His mother was her only child. Jamie, not yet two years old, was the sole survivor of a motorway accident outside of town. The family were to spend Christmas with her before his father took an overseas posting.

"Granny!" His hand shook her sleeve. The insistent voice brought her back to the present day. "Granny, when will we get the Christmas tree?"

"Nunky Joe is bringing it tonight. A real live Christmas tree, just your size. Later on you can plant it in the garden like your mother did with her first Christmas tree."

Jamie's eyes widened. "Did she, Granny? Which was Mummy's Christmas tree?"

Mrs. Hazeltine led him to a tall cypress at the side of the veranda. Jamie stood for a long time looking up through the branches to the spiky crown. His next question was a surprise.

"Granny, can we decorate Mummy's tree? If she looks down from heaven she'll know we are thinking about her."

Mrs. Hazeltine looked up into the tree. She blinked tears away and swallowed the lump in her throat. “We’ll ask Nunky Joe, Jamie.”

Nunky Joe brought a just-right tree for Jamie and a stool for him to stand on while he placed the angel on the top. While he strung the tinsel, hung the cookies and clipped the candles to the branches, Mrs. Hazeltine asked Nunky Joe about the tree outside.

When Nunky Joe hunkered down to admire Jamie’s tree he said, “Jamie, at the weekend I will bring Auntie Weeza and the children and we’ll see what we can do with your Mummy’s tree.”

Auntie Weeza brought the children in the car. From the trunk they took a huge box of fairy lights and the biggest star Jamie had ever seen. Nunky Joe drove a cherry picker and brought a few ladders. Mrs. Hazeltine cut a loaf or two of sandwiches, loaded trays with cakes and cookies and poured a gallon of lemonade. It was a very busy day and in the afternoon Nunky Joe took Jamie up in the cherry picker to place the star at the top of the tree.

While it grew dark they sat on the veranda drinking cups of soup, finishing off the sandwiches and cakes. At last it was dark enough. Auntie Weeza turned off the house lights. Jamie threw the switch. The fairy lights flickered and glowed, the star blazed at the sky and the silvered tree stood alone in the dark garden. Jamie drew a deep breath.

“Thank you, thank you everybody.”

He flung his arms around his grandmother. “Thank you, Granny.”

In a whisper he added, “Thank you, Jesus. On Christmas day the tree will be all yours. Please let Mummy look at her tree tonight and know that we love her and we miss her, too.”

REMEMBER ME?

WS

Hi there, all my friends now scattered abroad. Christmas greetings!

I wanted to send you a card so you would realise that I was thinking of you today. Then I thought how many cards it would take and just how special each of you is. I wanted to find a unique card to suit each one of you, and then I thought of how I would have to send them almost to the four corners of the earth. I became overwhelmed. What a task and what cost!

My mind went back to those years when I sat with my long list that had become my 'prayer list' of names and addresses, with a pile of cards, and reminisced as I wrote each one, thinking of the good friend it was going to. No time to dream of a 'White Christmas' I had never known, but lots of precious memories of happy days with you.

Those Christmas eve's when we banded together and went carolling and then sat, worn out, in the church hall laughing and joking and snacking until we greeted Him at midnight as the angels had. Then the Christmas day services when we hoarsely sang those carols again and were reminded of the real meaning of Christmas by our Pastor. There were also those times coming up to Christmas when some would arrive unannounced at our door and we would just sit and 'chew the fat.'

Don't you wish it was all still happening? Who wants a 'White Christmas' anyway? If we could just be together again to celebrate our Saviour's birth. I can hear some of you saying, "The date's not right, you know." So what? Jesus really came, born of a virgin in Bethlehem. Not like Santa, Rudolph and Frosty, who are just imaginary. Jesus is still the real reason for this season of happiness.

My goodness, just look how time flies! These cards should have been in the post weeks ago. They'll never get there on time now and I've not even started to fill in the first one! What now?

That's why I am sending you this email, to wish you a very special Christmas as Jesus lives in your heart, and may the coming year be filled with His peace, His presence and His provision, as always.

May the very God of peace bless you with tremendous blessings now and always, and may His grace abound to you.

Remember me?

"For unto you is born this day in the city of David, a SAVIOUR, which is CHRIST THE LORD"

Luke 2:11 KJV

JESSICA'S GIFT

FDS

The little girl opened the door a tiny crack and peered through. The old lady sat in the big chair beside the window. Her eyes were closed. Carefully Jessica edged the door a little wider and crept through. Holding a tiny parcel behind her back with one hand, she used the other to once more close the door.

For some minutes she stood beside the chair, studying her grandmother's face. The lines were deeply etched, mouth and cheeks sagging in relaxation. Jessica reached a delicate hand and brushed a strand of grey hair from the eye nearest her. Granny's hands fluttered, her mouth firmed and her eyes opened. She took a moment to focus, then with obvious pleasure greeted her granddaughter.

"Well, good morning, Jessie-girl. This is a lovely surprise. What are you doing up so early? You are looking very pretty today."

Jessie did a quick pirouette so that Granny could see her finery all the way round.

“I wanted to be the first to wish you happy Christmas and give you my present.” She held out the brightly wrapped parcel, explaining, “I chose it just for you and I wrapped it myself.”

“Thank you, my dear.”

Her grandmother pulled gently at the sticky tape until the paper fell away. In her palm she held a tiny plastic manger scene. She looked from the cheap toy to the expectant face.

“Jessie, my dear, thank you. You couldn’t have given me anything nicer.” She placed the ornament on the windowsill beside her. “Will you bring me my Bible please.”

Jessica handed the Bible to her grandmother, holding it with both hands. While her grandmother found the place, Jessica snuggled down on the rug next to Granny’s slippered feet. Alternately reading and explaining Granny’s soft voice recounted the Christmas story.

Together they followed Mary and Joseph down to Bethlehem town. As Mary sank into the hay in the stable, Jessie snuggled closer to Granny's legs and tucked her thumb into her mouth. They visited the shepherds on the hillside, and sat completely still and quiet to listen to the angel's song. After some minutes Jessie took her thumb from her mouth and looked up into her grandmother's face. Her voice was a sigh of contentment.

"Oh, Granny, that was the most beautiful song!"

Her grandmother smiled.

"Yes, Jessie-girl, the most beautiful song about the very best gift of all – the gift of God's Son."

With an effort she pulled the four-year-old onto her knee, placing her Bible on the child's lap.

"And now, Jessie, I have a gift for you. It is the very best gift I could ever give you. I want you to read it every day."

“But, Gran,” Jessie started to protest. Her hands closed around the edges of the Book, afraid it would fall.

“But nothing, Jessie. I won’t need it anymore. I’m going to live with Jesus.”

“Thank you, Gran.” Jessie leaned into her grandmother’s embrace.

Jessie stirred. She was sitting in the old armchair beside the window. A tattered Bible lay on her lap. A faded ornament stood on the windowsill. She lifted the Bible and looked at it, thinking “Thank you, Granny. It is still the best gift I have ever received. For sixty years you have shared with me the truths about the Saviour, God’s gift of His Son, His love and His forgiveness. For sixty years I have shared your gift of the beautiful angel’s song. Thank you, Gran.”

She remembered her mother coming into Granny’s room, taking the Bible from Jessie’s grasp, lifting the little girl from her grandmother’s arms. It was some time before she understood their tears, before she cried into the pages of her Book, and the words at the funeral comforted her: 'I go to prepare a place for you...that where I am, there you may be also.'

She smoothed her hands across the worn cover and murmured again, "Thank you, Granny."

"I am the resurrection and the life: he that believeth in Me, though he were dead, yet shall he live;
And whosoever liveth and believeth in Me shall never die."
John 11:25, 26 KJV

HOW FAR IS IT TO BETHLEHEM?

FDS

"Don't fuss, he says, don't fuss! These men are all the same. I said to him, Heli, surely you know how far it is from Nazareth to Bethlehem. And Mary is heavy with this child. How can a mother not worry about her child? And her first baby – who will be there when her time comes? I said to Joseph," her voice softened momentarily, "Joseph, he is a good man, very kind, very gentle." Her tones grew strident again. "But he is a man! I said to him, who will be there to help my daughter when the baby comes? And do you know what he said, Heli? He said, 'Mama, don't worry, I will be there.' Don't worry! What does a carpenter know about birth? How can I not worry, Heli, how can I not worry?"

Heli waved his hand deprecatingly. "Mama," he began. His voice was soothing but she was not soothed.

"What if the baby comes while they are travelling?" she burst out. "What if she has a fall? What if there is nowhere for them to stay in Bethlehem? What if..."

"What if...what if...what if..." Heli interrupted her impatiently. "Is not this the way of our people? We are not Gentiles who have no gods to help them. Is not our God the living God? Did not our daughter say that this child is promised of God? That He will deliver Israel? Woman, you fuss for nothing! Our daughter is young but she is strong. You have taught her well. She is prepared. And Joseph is a good man. He will take care of her – of her and the baby. He will provide for them and he will protect them. It is not his fault they have had to travel to Bethlehem at this time. You can blame Caesar for that! Besides, have you forgotten that the angel of the Lord spoke first to Mary and then to Joseph about this baby? If it was important for God – blessed be His name – to send His angel at that time, do you doubt that He will send His angel to watch over them now?"

Red-faced after his impassioned and unaccustomed speech, Heli strode from the room. His wife picked up the bowls and plates used for their meal and carried them to the basin of water to wash them. She was subdued but still the worry lines etched her eyes and mouth. She sank to the floor, lifting her eyes and hands upward. Her tears flowed freely. Her voice was low, imploring.

"Lord, look upon your handmaid with mercy. I understand, Lord, that this is the child of Your promise, that according to Your word Mary had to go to Bethlehem because that is where the baby must be born. But Lord, forgive my importunity. Mary is my child. Can a woman forget the child to whom she gave suck? It is not so many years since she lay at my breast. I know that you are the great God, the only God, and that you have chosen Israel to be your people. Look upon me, Lord, a daughter of your people, Israel, and pity me. It is so far from Bethlehem to Nazareth. How will I know? How can I be sure?"

She heard the words as a whisper, dropped into her mind. The worry lines smoothed; her face, her hands, her body relaxed.

"Listen for the angel song, my daughter. You will hear the angels sing."

A GIFT REFUSED

WS

It was Christmas eve and Ned and Betty's dining table was elaborately furnished with dainties. The gaily decorated Christmas tree stood in a corner of the lounge section of the room. There were no gifts at the tree for Santa had not yet been. The lounge/dining room was festooned with brightly coloured decorations. Everything was very festive and friends dropped in to celebrate.

Mr. and Mrs. Liqourice were first to arrive. Her naturally white hair was coloured in streaks of orange and green to match her new evening gown. They stayed just long enough to enjoy a drink and a brief chat with their hosts before going on to the Christmas Ball.

As they left, Ernie and his lady arrived in their finery as well. They were also on their way to the Christmas Ball in the city hall. Ernie and Joan were old friends and lingered longer chewing the fat over last Christmases. While they were there the father and brother of Felix, Ned's current apprentice jockey, dropped in for a free drink. The brother had already imbibed too much and soon became cantankerous, calling Betty a few rude names. Ned stood to his feet, indignant.

"You'll take that back and apologise or you'll have me to deal with!" he cried.

"Which army will help you?" the brother replied.

At that Ernie stood to his feet, being younger than Ned. "I will."

A scuffle ensued and the father and brother were thrown out of the house. There was blood on Ernie's white tuxedo, which Betty tearfully cleaned, thanking him for his defence of her honour.

Once all was settled again the festivities continued and Ernie and Joan went on to the ball.

On Christmas day Felix came to the house. He had exercised, cleaned and fed the thoroughbreds as always. His arms were full of beautifully wrapped gifts which he had bought for the family.

"I know you had nothing to do with last night's furore." Ned told him, "but I have decided to approach the Jockey Club to find you a new trainer as a result. Because of this I am afraid we cannot accept your gifts."

Christmas was really spoiled for all of us.

Often at Christmas I recall this incident and wonder. Our family were only Christians in name at that time and I was just a child. It may have been different if we had really known the Christ.

As I ponder this occasion once more, I think of the great number of people that I have met over the years whose refusal to accept God's great Gift at Christmas is based on some tragedy that happened in their lives: a loved one killed in an accident at Christmas, caused by a drunken driver; or one who died of an incurable disease; or another who was imprisoned for a crime he committed.

Why didn't God stop these things happening? I am not able to answer every specific case, not knowing the detailed facts, but I can say that the God of the Bible is not someone who wished evil on anyone. Jesus said, "The thief only comes to steal and kill and destroy, but I have come to give to each of you a full and satisfying life." Peter, telling of the results of God's gift at Christmas in the home of Cornelius, said, "Remember how God anointed Jesus of Nazareth with the Holy Ghost and power. He went about doing good and healing all that were oppressed by the devil."

God's great Gift at Christmas was His only true Son, Jesus the Christ, who demonstrated what God wanted for us and then gave His life on the cross for us. Ned and Betty's family did not gain any benefits from Felix' gifts because they refused them. In fact, they never even knew what they had missed.

You too will never know the benefits of God's great Christmas Gift if you refuse it. Why don't you 'taste and see that the Lord is good'? Although God's Gift was given over two thousand years ago, each of us can still receive the gift and its benefits today. Make room in your heart for Jesus today and receive the gift of life.

"Have you any room for Jesus,
He who bore your load of sin –
As He knocks and asks admission,
Sinner, will you let Him in?

Room for Jesus, King of Glory,

Hasten now His word obey

Swing your heart's door widely open,

Bid Him enter while you may.

D. W. Whittle

COUNCIL OF THREE

FDS

A star fell from heaven. A ripple of shock ran through the watching crowd. "The anointed cherub?" questioned one of another, and was answered by a barely perceptible nod.

From the roiling darkness at the foot of the throne a spirit stood indignant. "It's not fair!" he proclaimed and plunged after the first fallen. Others followed.

The Holy Council of Three discussed the future of the footstool, now an uninhabited chaos of darkness.

"Let us make man," said the First.

"A little lower than the angels," added the Second, also known as the Word. "But with the intelligence to make decisions."

They discussed their plans in all the infinitesimal detail of the cosmos. They discussed the danger of the once anointed cherub, now become the Evil One, who would certainly oppose the presentation of his former home to a lesser creation. No aspect was forgotten. No particular was ignored. At length the Second stood to his feet.

“When that time comes,” he stated, “I will be ready. I will go.”

“And I with you,” added the Third.

“Keep in close touch,” was the request of the First. “Shall we begin?”

The Third spread himself across the face of the dark, churning waters and hovered, brooding.

The First commanded, “Let there be light!”

The Word created. Without him was nothing made that was made.

They saw the light was good, and the First made a division between the light and the darkness.

So with immeasurable care and infinite variety the earth was created a home for man. With each step taken the Three examined it carefully to see that it was good. And then the work was done; the time had come to make a man. "...in our image..." was the command. The Word took the clay in his fingers and so lovingly – so carefully – he pinched and smoothed and shaped. Like a potter turning a cup on a wheel, he removed the small impurities. Until he had a perfect man. The Three examined the work of his hands. It was good. The Third stooped and breathed into the nostrils of the man the breath of life. And man became a living soul.

So the story of the man began. He was given dominion over all the earth, to care for it, to multiply and fill the earth.

Just as the Three had foreseen, the Evil One contested man's right to live upon the earth. He entered the garden home of man and made an insinuating accusation against the Three. Accepting his accusation, the man lost to the Evil One his dominion of the earth. The Three intervened, removing the man from the next danger, offering a means of continued communication with them.

Through many troubled years the Three watched over the man and the sons of men, calling out their warnings, intervening here and there. They were cursed and sometimes blessed; disregarded often, occasionally obeyed. To chosen man the Three gave warning of the years ahead; promises of a ransom from the Evil One. The warnings were largely disregarded, the promises decried. Until the First said, “It is time.”

The Second laid aside his divinity, stepped into the womb of a young girl chosen by the Third. The angels stood on tiptoe, waiting for his birth. This was the Beloved Son who would defeat the Evil One. The Beloved Son who would stand between the Evil One and the sons of men, offering them an eternity spent in the presence of the Three, or an eternal denial of their glory and their love.

The Baby was born. The Light of heaven broke through upon the earth. The words of a prophet echoed through the universe: “For unto us a Child is born ... and the government shall be upon his shoulder.” The angels appeared above the hills of Bethlehem to sing his glory. A bright new star appeared, signifying to wise men of the east the birth of a King.

The Baby was named Jesus, for “He would save his people from their sins.”

And this is the reason – the Person – we celebrate on Christmas day. The cross was yet to come. The resurrection lay ahead. Today we look forward to his soon return. And every year we celebrate again the promise of the first Christmas day.

RECORD OF BIRTH

Taken from the Gospels According to Luke and Matthew

The angel Gabriel was sent from God to a city of Galilee, named Nazareth; to a virgin engaged to a man whose name was Joseph, a descendant of David. The virgin's name was Mary. And the angel said to her, "Greetings, graciously accepted one, the Lord is with you. You are blessed among women."

Mary was troubled at this greeting, trying to imagine what the portent was.

"Do not be afraid, Mary," said the angel, "for you have found favour with God. You will conceive a child. You will give birth to a son, and you will name him Jesus. He shall be great. He shall be called the Son of the Highest, and the Lord God will give him the throne of his ancestor David. He shall reign over the house of Jacob forever. His kingdom shall be without end."

Mary asked, "How can this happen? I am not married."

To which the angel answered, "The Holy Ghost will come upon you, and the power of the Highest will over-shadow you, Therefore the baby that you bear shall be called the Son of God."

Mary answered, "I am the servant of the Lord. He may do with me as He wills."

And the angel left her.

Mary was engaged to Joseph, and before they were married she was found to be pregnant with the child of the Holy Ghost. Now Joseph was a just man, and did not wish to make a public example of Mary. While he was considering what he should do, the angel of the Lord appeared to him in a dream. “Joseph, descendant of David,” he said, “don’t be afraid to take Mary as your wife – the baby she is carrying is the child of the Holy Ghost. She will give birth to a son, and you will name him Jesus, for he shall save his people from their sins. You will recall the prophecy spoken by the Lord through the prophet Isaiah, *‘Behold, a virgin shall be with child, and shall bring forth a son, and his name shall be called Emmanuel, which being interpreted is God with us.’*

When Joseph awoke, he took Mary to be his wife.

In those days Caesar Augustus required that all the world should be taxed. So everyone went to be taxed. Because Joseph was of the lineage of David, he was required to go from Nazareth to the city of David, the city Bethlehem, with his wife Mary, to be taxed. While they were there the baby was born. They had been unable to find any shelter but a stable, so Mary put the baby in a manger.

During that night an angel appeared to some shepherds out in the fields, watching over their flocks. The angel said, “Do not be afraid. Tonight I bring news of great joy to all people. Today, in the city of David, a Saviour is born, who is Christ the Lord. As a sign to you, you will find the baby wrapped in swaddling clothes, lying in a manger.” And suddenly the sky was filled with angels praising God and saying, “Glory to God in the highest!”

CHRISTMAS LIGHT

FDS

Along the rooflines sharp and bright,
Outlining Santa and his sleigh,
Myriad lights blink on and off.
CD's their carols play.

With angel lights the gardens glow,
From window shines a star,
And all mankind will come to see
This glory, from the car.

With oohs and aahs appreciate
The artistry of night.
By day the colours dominate
The senses with delight.

But follow the star – that shining star –
Out to the dark hillside
Where shepherds once their flocks did keep,
In folds their sheep did hide.

Tonight the shepherd sleeps at home,
His sheep lie far away;
Alpaca's guard the clust'ring flocks
To keep the fox at bay.

He counts the dollars in his bank
Before he counts his sheep.
The poddy lamb's the children's pet
For them to watch and keep.

But on those darkened fields of yore
The door of God ope'd wide,
The light of glory shining through
To bathe the dark hillside.

The praise of angels rent the skies
With comfort and great cheer:
"To you, in David's town, is born
The Saviour – Christ is here!"

The angel left, the heaven shut,
The shepherds ran to see
If this great news was true indeed,
And stayed to bow the knee.

The wise men led by star so bright
It drew them from their land,
With gifts for the King it heralded
As they did understand.

We light our world electrically
But don’t dispel the dark;
We sing the song the angels sang,
But do we miss the mark?

The Light of the world is Jesus Christ –
He is the Christmas Light –
He ope’d the door of heaven’s grace
When He came that Christmas night.

He came with the gift of God's great love.

He came with His sinlessness.

He came to a race of sin-sick men

To heal, forgive and bless.

And we took that glorious Light of God

And hung Him upon a cross;

We bowed in mock humility

To aggravate our loss.

"Father, your work is done!" He cried,

"Forgive them, for they don't know ..."

And we raise our cup of Yuletide cheer

In determined electric glow.

Once more the door will open wide,
The King of heaven will come
With His armies and with His ransomed bride,
To bring His people home.

No angel song, but a trumpet call;
No star, but a great earthquake
When His feet touch down on Olive's Mount –
The earth will reel and shake.

He will rule the land with an iron rod,
The Lion of Judah now.
Ev'ry eye will see the Lamb of God,
And every knee will bow.

Out on the hills of Bethlehem
The shepherd will guard his sheep;
Sing of the night when the Light of God
Was born while men were asleep.

The watchmen are keeping a watch tonight
As they read from the written word:
"He is coming!" they call with insistent voice,
"Are you ready to meet the Lord?"

AS we come to the end of another year may we carry the reflections of Christmas, the joy of Christmas, the GIFT of Christmas, into the year that lies ahead.

The Gospel of John records the words of Jesus, “I go to prepare a place for you, ... and I will come again, and receive you unto myself, that where I am you may be also.”

Paul’s words to the Thessalonian church apply as much to all of us now as to them:

“And the Lord direct your hearts unto the love of God, and into the patient waiting for Christ.”

Until He comes .....

www.ingramcontent.com/pod-product-compliance
Ingram Content Group UK Ltd.
Pitfield, Milton Keynes, MK11 3LW, UK
UKHW020236250726
13967UKWH00001B/400